Any time of year, **Mammal Tracks and Scat: Life-Size Pocket Guide** helps you discover which mammal has left tracks or scat right where you are.

You can use **Mammal Tracks and Scat: Life-Size Pocket Guide** alone, but it is most effective when used with *Mammal Tracks and Scat: Life-Size Tracking Guide*, which has more detailed information.

This guide emphasizes the SHAPE and SIZE of the tracks and scat — and you see **first-of-its-kind** __Track Key__ (pages 3-6) and a **first-of-its-kind** __Scat Key__ (page 2

Identification is easiest when the tracks are **CLEAR**. Look for animal prints on a firm a log or rock (in winter), wet sand or dense mud. Then, the footprints are more "true t closer to the measurements noted throughout this guide. In dense material, feeling tr may help you determine, for example, the number of toes or whether there are claws. "tree tracks," which may look like animal tracks, but were really caused by snow falling

For tracks, the dimensions refer to the size of the **hind** feet. The newer the track or sc chances of accurate identification. Older tracks have often been aged by wind, water o snow, by warmer weather. This will make the track bigger than the dimensions listed in Older scat has sometimes been altered by moisture, mold or by exposure to the sun.

If there is a trail of prints, see the __Track Pattern Key__ (pages 7 & 8) and keep looking for clear tracks.

This **TRACK KEY** is divided into two broad categories:

TRACKS ARE ABOUT THE <u>SAME SIZE</u>

BECAUSE THE FRONT and HIND FEET ARE ALMOST EQUAL IN SIZE.

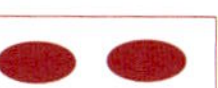

(PAGE 4)

Often, in tracks about the same size, **only the tracks of the back feet are visible** because the mammal's hind feet stepped right into where the front feet had just been.

OR

TRACKS ARE <u>NOT</u> THE <u>SAME SIZE</u>

BECAUSE THE HIND FEET ARE ALWAYS BIGGER — OFTEN WITH MORE TOES.

(PAGES 5 & 6)

Often, in tracks that are not the same size, the bigger tracks **don't cover** the front tracks because the hind feet usually do not step into where the front feet had just been.

In addition, this key considers the number of toes, the presence of claws, the track pattern, and the track size and shape. The range of the **STRADDLE (width of the pattern)** is noted next to the illustration of each track (pages 9-27) and the average straddle is noted in the Track Pattern Key (pages 7-8).

straddle

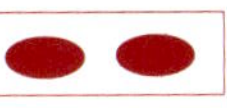

TRACK KEY: SAME SIZE

PRINTS ARE ABOUT THE SAME SIZE

	Tracks	Page	Track Patterns
(A)	**4 Toes** With an "X" across the paw print and with claws		
	Gray Fox	9	
	Red Fox	9	
	Coyote	10	
	Gray Wolf.	10	
(B)	**4 Toes** Without an "X" and no claws		
	Bobcat	11	
	Mountain Lion	11	
(C)	**5 Toes** Without an "X" and with claws		
	Weasel	12	
	Mink	12	
	Marten	13	
	Fisher.	13	
	Otter (webbed).	14	
(D)	**Hoof**		
	Deer	15	
	Moose	15	

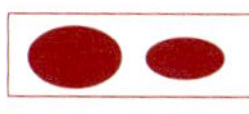

TRACK KEY: NOT the SAME SIZE

PRINTS ARE NOT THE SAME SIZE

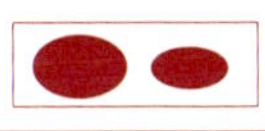

	Tracks	Page	Track Patterns
E	All four prints together (**small** tracks) **Shrew**. . . . . **Mouse** . . . . **Chipmunk** . . . . **Red Squirrel** . . . . **Gray Squirrel**.	16 16 16 17 17	
F	All four prints together (**large** tracks) **Cottontail Rabbit**. . . . **Snowshoe Hare**.	18 19	
G	Look like human hands **Raccoon**	20	
H	Large opposable thumb marks **Opossum**.	21	
I	Webbing between the toes **Beaver**	22	

TRACK KEY: NOT the SAME SIZE

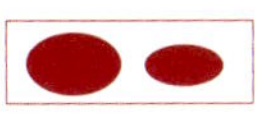

PRINTS ARE NOT THE SAME SIZE

	Tracks	Page	Track Patterns
J	Look like human feet (the bigger tracks) **Bear**	23	
K	Long, inward pointing toe marks **Porcupine**	24	
L	Long and skinny toe marks **Muskrat** . . . . (found near water)	25	
M	Long and curvy toe marks **Woodchuck**	26	
N	Different from all others **Skunk**.	27	

TRACK PATTERN KEY

This key is most helpful when there is a trail of prints. Keep following the trail to discover which one of the four patterns shown below is the closest match. Measure the straddle and compare it to the average measurements listed below (ranges are on pages 9-27). The straddle will be wider in deep snow, mud, or sand. To learn more about the animal's behavior, look at the spacing between prints. The faster the animal is moving, the bigger the space (for example, the *Bounding* pattern shows that the speed is increasing — left to right).

1. *WALKING AND TROTTING*: TRACKS ROUGHLY IN A STRAIGHT LINE (**Similar** size feet)

The bigger the mammal, the larger the straddle, and the bigger the "zig-zag" (illustrated by the arrows).

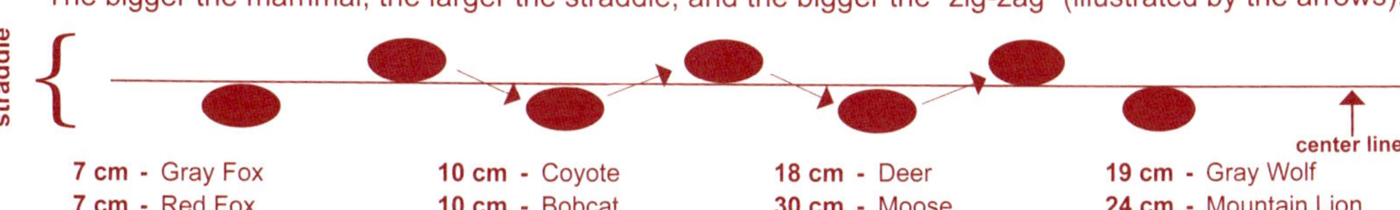

7 cm - Gray Fox
7 cm - Red Fox
10 cm - Coyote
10 cm - Bobcat
18 cm - Deer
30 cm - Moose
19 cm - Gray Wolf
24 cm - Mountain Lion

2. *BOUNDING*: PAIRS OF TRACKS AT A DIAGONAL — SOMETIMES 3 TRACKS (**Similar** size feet)

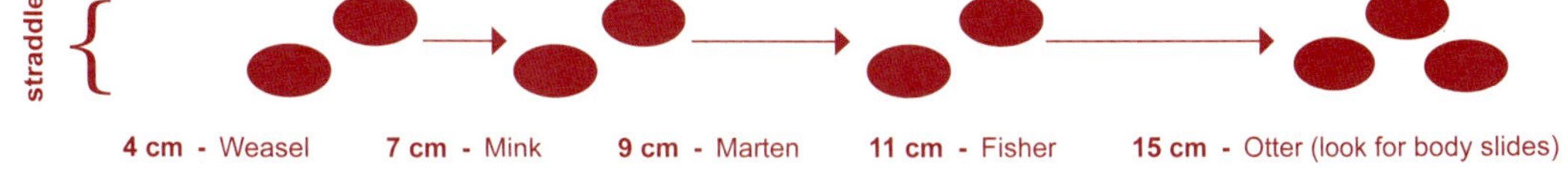

4 cm - Weasel
7 cm - Mink
9 cm - Marten
11 cm - Fisher
15 cm - Otter (look for body slides)

3. ***HOPPING***--A GROUP OF FOUR TRACKS

(**Not the same** size feet). Sometimes, groups of four tracks may merge into one. This may look like Pattern 1, but without the zig-zag.

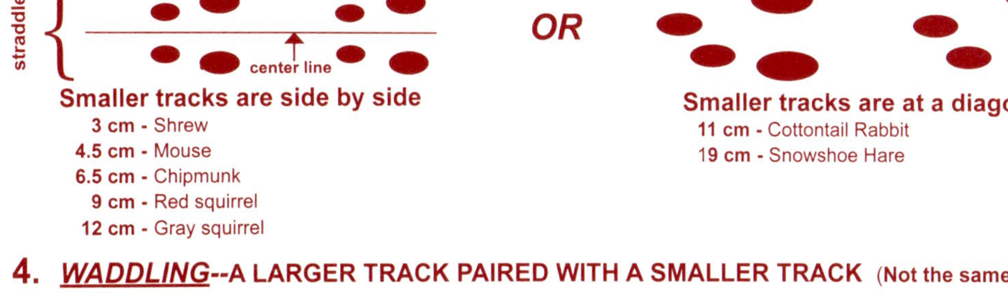

Smaller tracks are side by side

- **3 cm** - Shrew
- **4.5 cm** - Mouse
- **6.5 cm** - Chipmunk
- **9 cm** - Red squirrel
- **12 cm** - Gray squirrel

Smaller tracks are at a diagonal

- **11 cm** - Cottontail Rabbit
- **19 cm** - Snowshoe Hare

4. ***WADDLING***--A LARGER TRACK PAIRED WITH A SMALLER TRACK

(**Not the same** size feet)

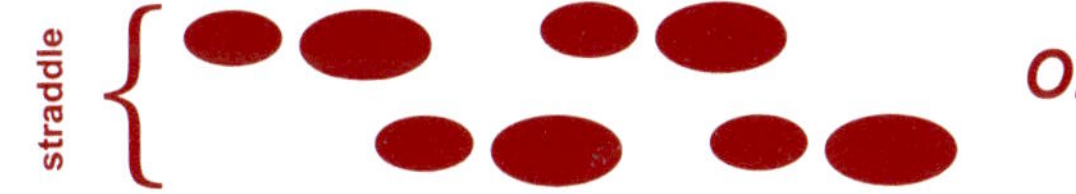

Larger tracks are in front/behind smaller ones

- **9-10 cm** - Muskrat, Opossum, Skunk or Woodchuck
- **17 cm** - Porcupine
- **21 cm** - Beaver
- **28 cm** - Bear

Larger tracks are next to smaller ones

- **11 cm** - Raccoon

GRAY FOX

STRADDLE: 5-10 cm

TRACK: 4-5 cm (L)
4-5 cm (W)

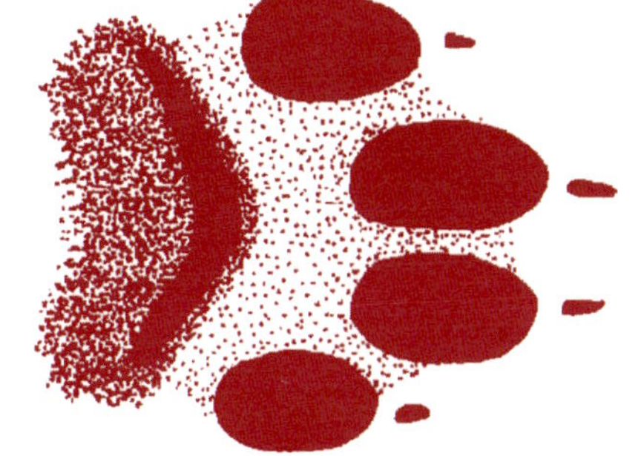

RED FOX

STRADDLE: 5-10 cm

TRACK: 5-7 cm (L)
4-5 cm (W)

(L) = Length
(W) = Width

Similar Size Tracks	4 Toes	*"X"* *Across the Paw Print*	*Claws* *Rare for Gray Fox*	*Key ---- Page 4* 

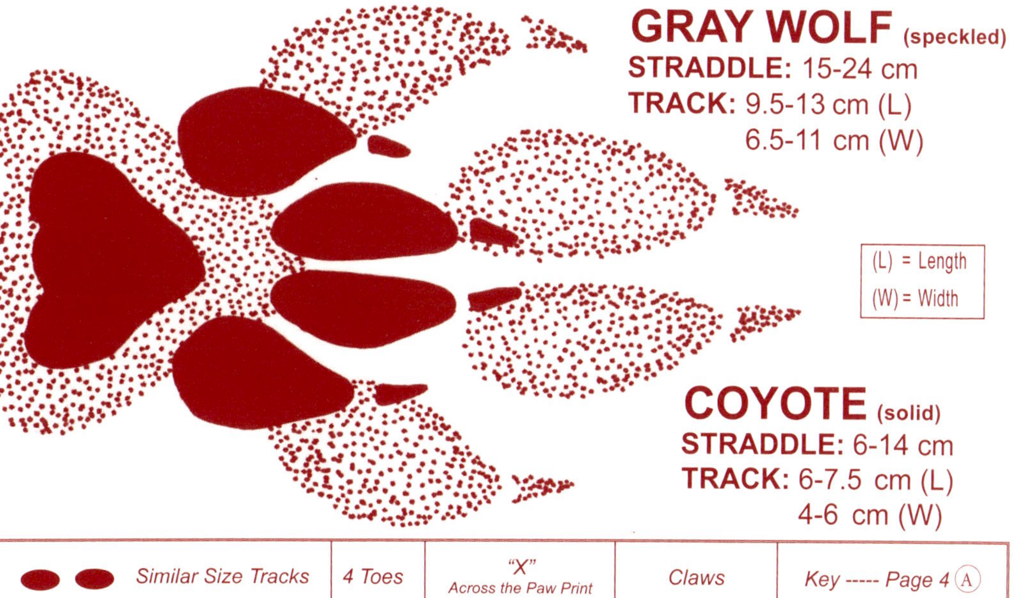

GRAY WOLF (speckled)

STRADDLE: 15-24 cm

TRACK: 9.5-13 cm (L)
6.5-11 cm (W)

(L) = Length
(W) = Width

COYOTE (solid)

STRADDLE: 6-14 cm

TRACK: 6-7.5 cm (L)
4-6 cm (W)

Similar Size Tracks	*4 Toes*	*"X" Across the Paw Print*	*Claws*	*Key ----- Page 4 (A)*

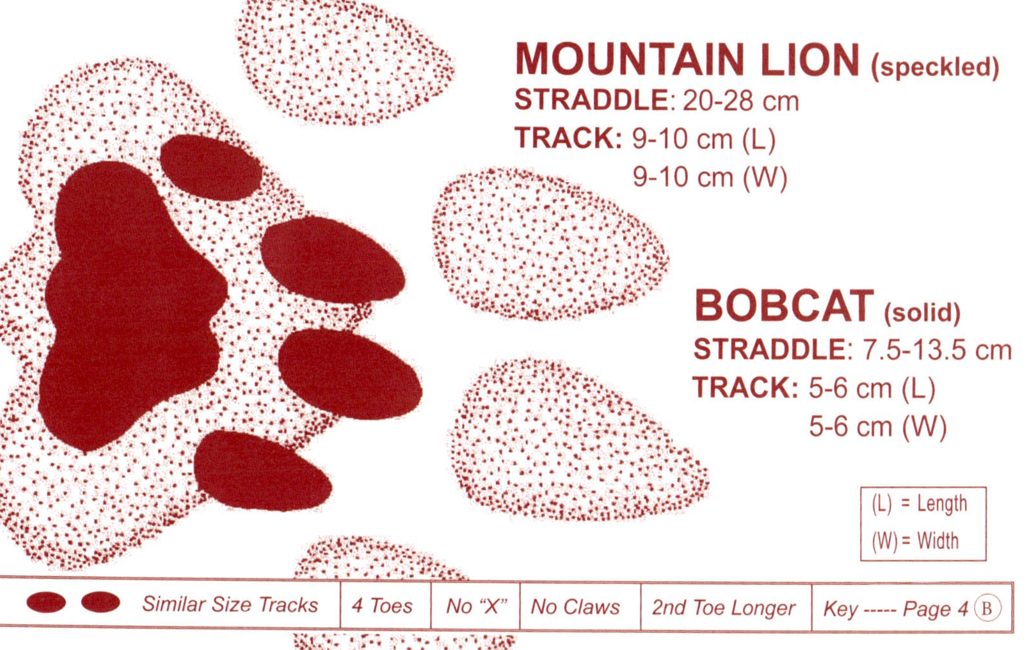

MOUNTAIN LION (speckled)

STRADDLE: 20-28 cm

TRACK: 9-10 cm (L)
9-10 cm (W)

BOBCAT (solid)

STRADDLE: 7.5-13.5 cm

TRACK: 5-6 cm (L)
5-6 cm (W)

(L) = Length
(W) = Width

Similar Size Tracks	*4 Toes*	*No "X"*	*No Claws*	*2nd Toe Longer*	*Key ----- Page 4* Ⓑ

WEASEL

STRADDLE:

LEAST 2-4 cm

SHORT-TAILED 2.5-5 cm

LONG-TAILED 4-7.5 cm

TRACK: 2 cm (L)
2 cm (W)

Mink

STRADDLE: 5-9 cm

TRACK: 3-5 cm (L)
3-5 cm (W)

(L) = Length
(W) = Width

Similar Size Tracks	*5 Toes*	*No "X"*	*Claws*	*Key ----- Page 4 Ⓒ*

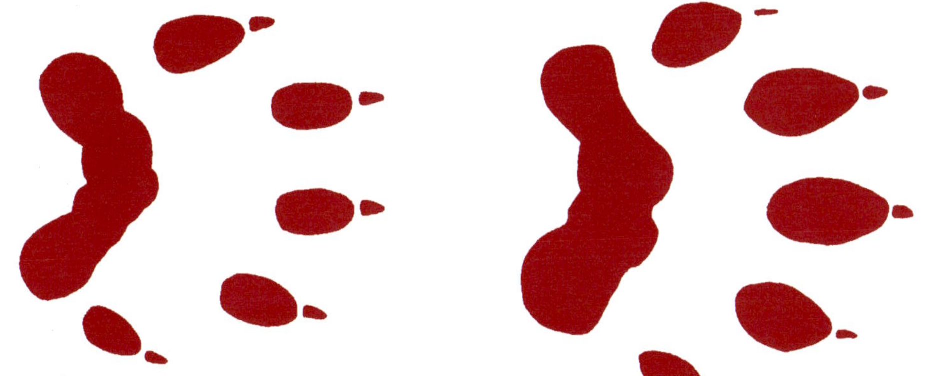

MARTEN

STRADDLE: 7.5-10.5 cm

TRACK: 4-7 cm (L)
3-5 cm (W)

FISHER

STRADDLE: 7.5-13.5 cm

TRACK: 5-7.5 cm (L)
5-7.5 cm (W)

(L) = Length
(W) = Width

	Similar Size Tracks	*5 Toes*	*No "X"*	*Claws*	*Key ----- Page 4* Ⓒ

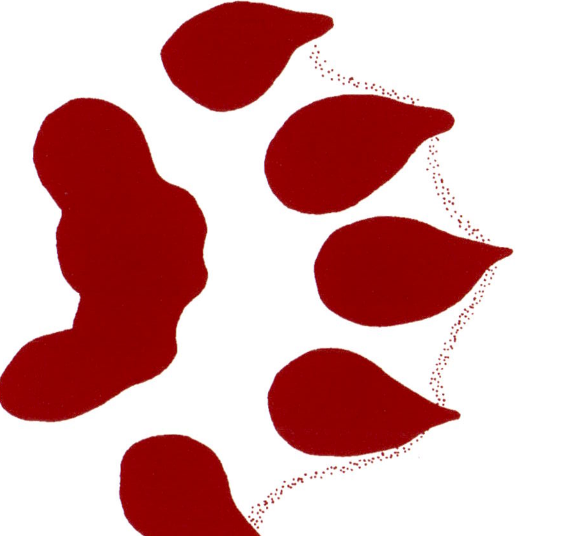

OTTER

STRADDLE: 10-19.5 cm

TRACK: 7-9.5 cm (L)
7-9.5 cm (W)

(L) = Length
(W) = Width

Similar Size Tracks	*5 Toes*	*No "X"*	*Webbed Toes*	*Claws*	*Key ----- Page 4 C*

MOOSE **(speckled)**
STRADDLE: 20.5-39 cm
TRACK: 10-17 cm (L)
9-14 cm (W)

DEER **(solid)**
STRADDLE: 12.5-24 cm
TRACK: 6-9 cm (L)
3-7 cm (W)

(L) = Length
(W) = Width

Similar Size Tracks	*Hoof*	*Key ----- Page 4 (D)*

SHREW

STRADDLE:
Less than 4 cm

TRACK: Hind Foot
5-6 mm (L)
5-6 mm (W)

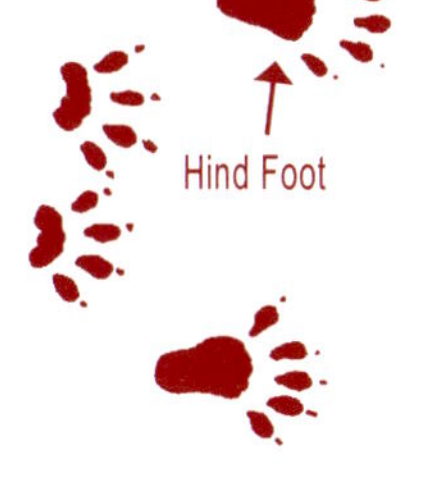

MOUSE

STRADDLE: 4-5 cm

TRACK: Hind Foot
9-12 mm (L)
10 mm (W)

CHIPMUNK

STRADDLE: 5-8 cm

TRACK: Hind Foot
2 cm (L)
1.5-2 cm (W)

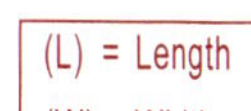

 *Tracks Not the Same Size* *Number of Toe — See above Illustrations*	*4 Tracks Together (Small)*	*Key ----- Page 5* Ⓔ

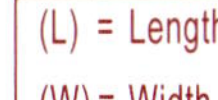

RED SQUIRREL

STRADDLE: 7.5-11 cm

TRACK: Hind Foot 2.5 cm (L)
2-3 cm (W)

GRAY SQUIRREL

STRADDLE: 10-14 cm

TRACK: Hind Foot 5 cm (L)
3-4 cm (W)

(L) = Length
(W) = Width

Tracks Not the Same Size *Bigger Tracks 5 Toes* *Smaller Tracks 4 Toes*	*4 Tracks Together (Small)*	*Key ----- Page 5* Ⓔ

COTTONTAIL RABBIT

STRADDLE: 10-13 cm

TRACK: Hind Foot 8.5 cm (L)
3-4 cm (W)

(L) = Length
(W) = Width

Tracks Not the Same Size	4 Tracks Together (Big)	Key ----- Page 5 (F)

SNOWSHOE HARE

STRADDLE: 17-21 cm

TRACK: Hind Foot 12 cm (L)
8 cm (W)

(L) = Length
(W) = Width

● ● Tracks Not the Same Size	4 Tracks Together (Big)	Key ----- Page 5 Ⓕ

RACCOON

STRADDLE: 8-14.5 cm

TRACK: Hind Foot 6-10 cm (L)
4-5 cm (W)

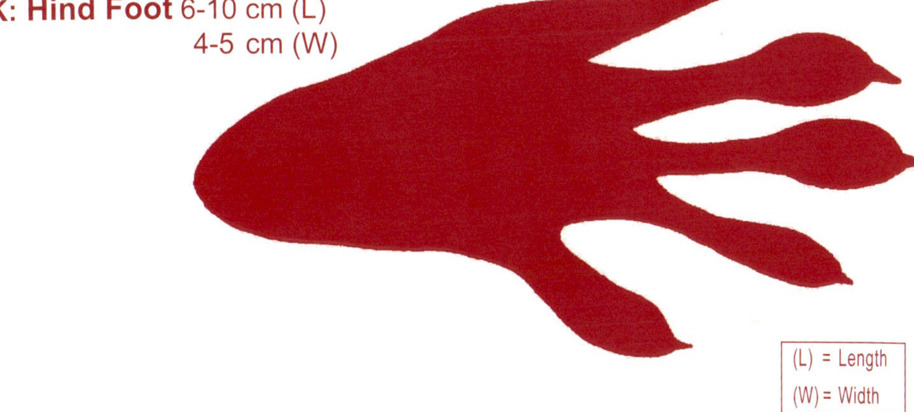

(L) = Length
(W) = Width

Tracks Not the Same Size *All Have 5 Toes*	*Look Like Human Hands*	*Key ----- Page 5* Ⓖ

OPOSSUM

STRADDLE: 6-11.5 cm

TRACK: Hind Foot 4.5-7 cm (L)
4-7 cm (W)

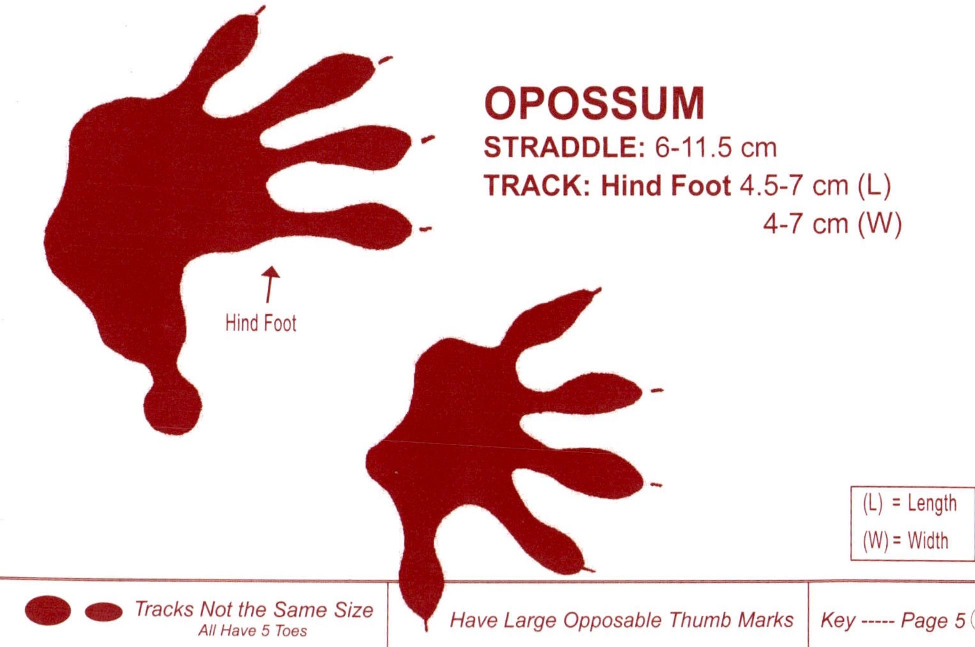

(L) = Length
(W) = Width

Tracks Not the Same Size *All Have 5 Toes*	*Have Large Opposable Thumb Marks*	*Key ----- Page 5* Ⓗ

BEAVER

STRADDLE: 15-27 cm

TRACK: Hind Foot:

12.5-17.5 cm (L)

8-13 cm (W)

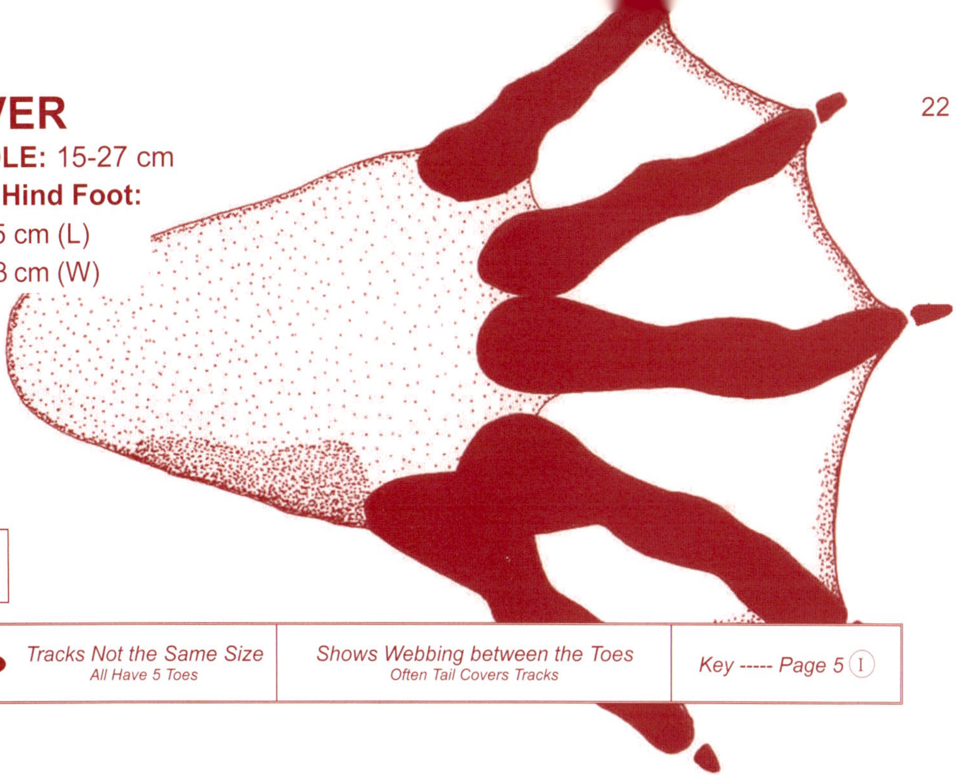

(L) = Length

(W) = Width

Tracks Not the Same Size *All Have 5 Toes*	Shows Webbing between the Toes *Often Tail Covers Tracks*	Key ----- Page 5 (I)

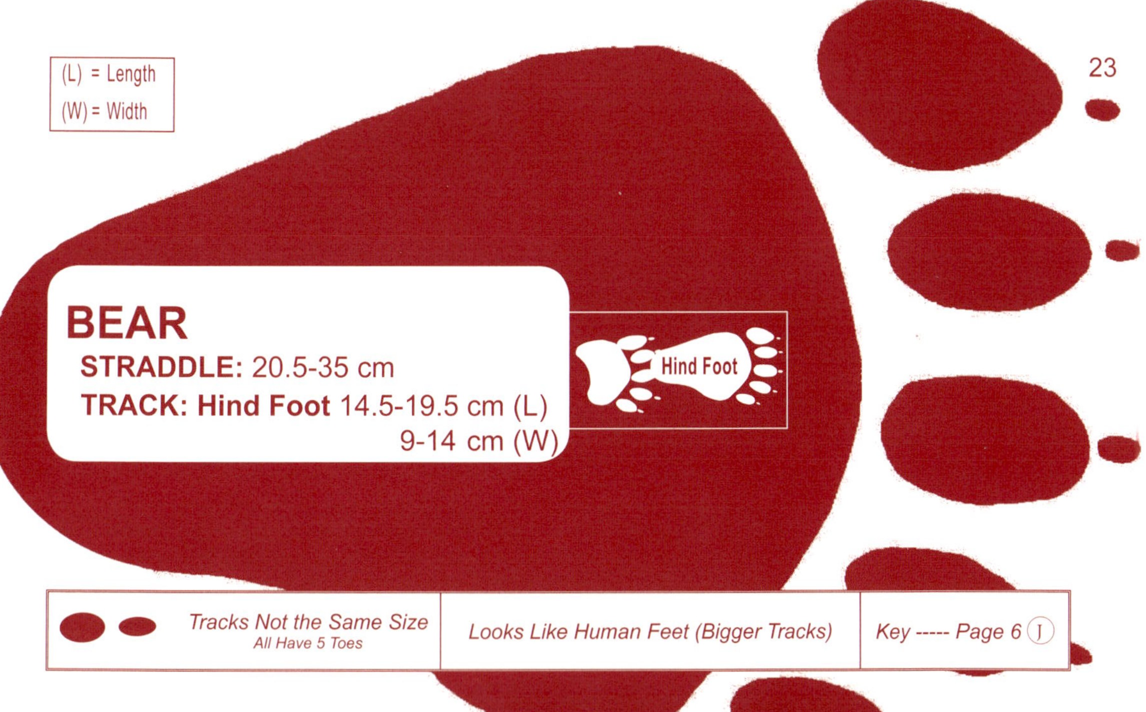

BEAR

STRADDLE: 20.5-35 cm

TRACK: Hind Foot 14.5-19.5 cm (L)
9-14 cm (W)

Tracks Not the Same Size *All Have 5 Toes*	*Looks Like Human Feet (Bigger Tracks)*	*Key ----- Page 6* (J)

(L) = Length
(W) = Width

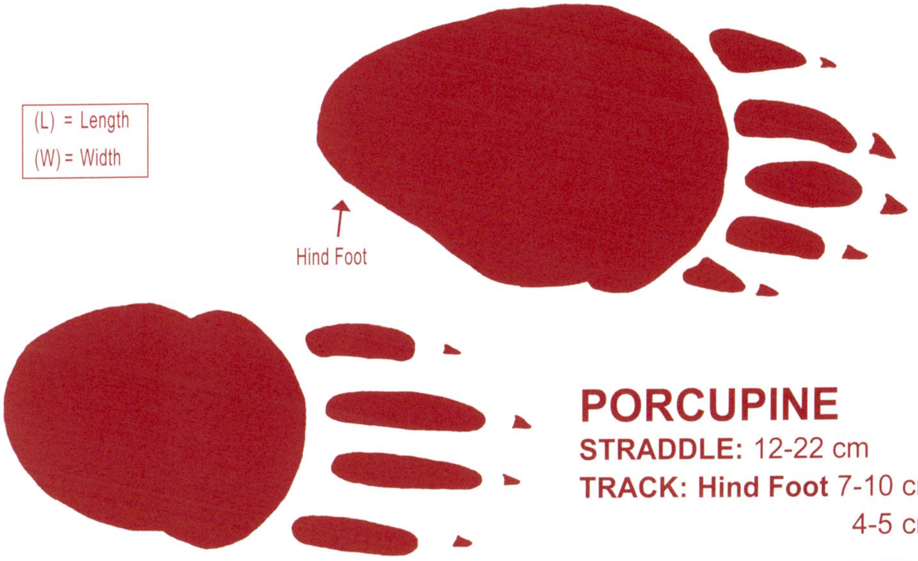

Hind Foot

PORCUPINE

STRADDLE: 12-22 cm

TRACK: Hind Foot 7-10 cm (L)
4-5 cm (W)

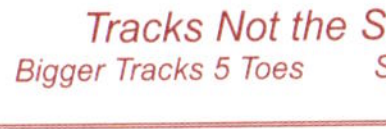

Tracks Not the Same Size *Bigger Tracks 5 Toes* *Smaller Tracks 4 Toes*	*Long Inward-Pointing Toe Marks* *Trail Used Repeatedly*	*Key ----- Page 6* Ⓚ

MUSKRAT

STRADDLE: 8-12.5cm

TRACK: Hind Foot 4-7 cm (L)
4-5 cm (W)

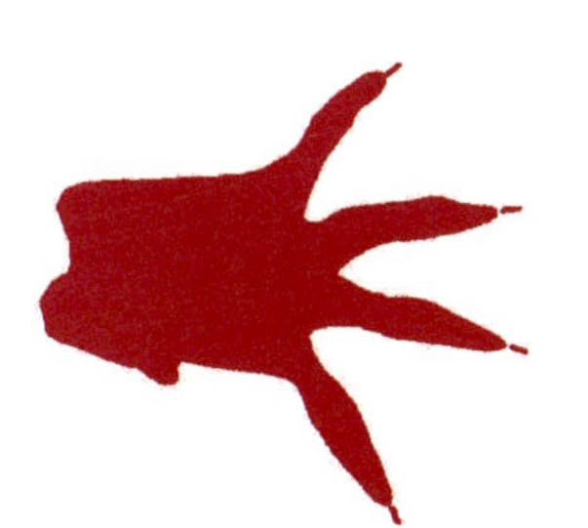

Hind Foot

(L) = Length
(W) = Width

Tracks Not the Same Size *Bigger Tracks 5 Toes* *Smaller Tracks 4 Toes*	*Long and Skinny Toe Marks*	*Key ----- Page 6* (L)

WOODCHUCK

STRADDLE: 8-14 cm

TRACK: Hind Foot 4.5-7 cm (L)
3.5-5 cm (W)

(L) = Length
(W) = Width

Tracks Not the Same Size *Bigger Tracks 5 Toes* *Smaller Tracks 4 Toes*	*Long and Curvy Toe Marks*	*Key ----- Page 6* Ⓜ

SKUNK

STRADDLE: 7-10.5 cm

TRACK: Hind Foot 4.-5 cm (L)
2.5-3 cm (W)

(L) = Length
(W) = Width

 *Tracks Not the Same Size* *All Have 5 Toes*	*Different from All Others*	*Key ----- Page 6* Ⓝ

SCAT KEY

Sphere OR Cylinder

SCAT KEY

	Sphere	Page
(A)	**Round**	
	Cottontail Rabbit	31
	Snowshoe Hare	31
(B)	**Elongated - Small**	
	Chipmunk	32
	Gray Squirrel	32
	Mouse	32
	Red Squirrel	32
	Shrew	32
(C)	**Elongated - Large**	
	Beaver	33
	Muskrat	33
	Porcupine	34
	Woodchuck	34
	Deer	35
	Moose	35

OR

	Cylinder	Page
(D)	**Pointed**	
	Gray fox	36
	Red fox	36
	Coyote	37
	Gray wolf	38
(E)	**Broken**	
	Bobcat	39
	Mountain Lion	39
(F)	**Twisted**	
	Fisher	40
	Marten	40
	Mink	40
	Weasel	40
(G)	**Blunt**	
	Bear	41
	Raccoon	41
(H)	**Misc.**	
	Opossum	42
	Skunk	42
	Otter	43

Spheres are typically left by herbivores, and cylinders are generally from carnivores. Herbivore scat mostly has plant matter. Carnivore scat can have plant matter, and animal matter such as bones, hair or feathers.

Scat is more challenging to identify than tracks. Scat varies depending upon what the animal ate and the time of year. During the spring, the scat from many animals that eat plants is loose and difficult to recognize. If you find both scat and tracks, it is much easier to determine what animal you are tracking. When possible, take the time to discover as many clues as you can. Don't forget to have fun being a detective!

What is most interesting about scat is the story it tells. By investigating, **not with your hand,** you may find bits of undigested food which will tell you something about the animal's habitat. Perhaps it had been in a berry patch, an apple orchard, or by an oak tree. If you find bones, feathers or hair, you might also be able to identify the animal that was the source of these body fragments.

The works of James Halfpenny, Paul Rezendes, Olaus Murie and Mark Elbroch were the basis for the scat measurements.

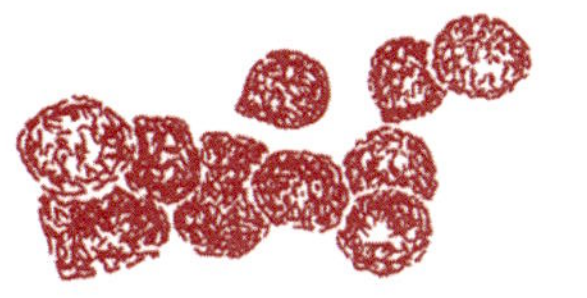

COTTONTAIL RABBIT

DIAMETER 0.5 cm
LENGTH 0.5 cm

Snowshoe hare scat usually contains compacted pieces of wood.

SNOWSHOE HARE

DIAMETER 0.8 cm
LENGTH 0.8 cm

 *Sphere*	*Round*	*Key ----- Page 29* 

Shrew scat usually contains insect fragments.

SHREW

DIAMETER	0.2 cm
LENGTH	0.5 cm

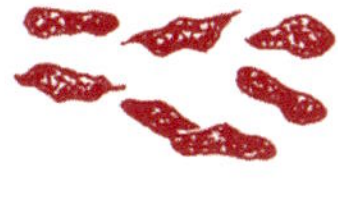

MOUSE

DIAMETER	0.2 cm
LENGTH	0.5 cm

CHIPMUNK

DIAMETER	0.2 cm
LENGTH	0.5 cm

RED SQUIRREL

DIAMETER	0.5 cm
LENGTH	0.8 cm

GRAY SQUIRREL

DIAMETER	0.5 cm
LENGTH	1.0 cm

 *Sphere*	*Elongated (Small)*	*Key ----- Page 29* (B)

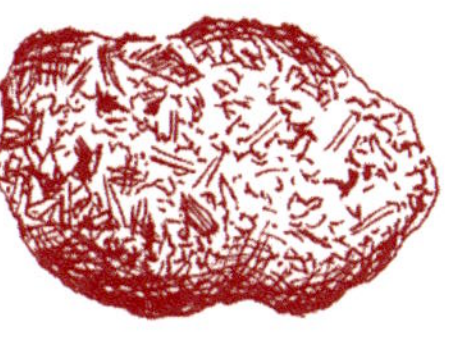

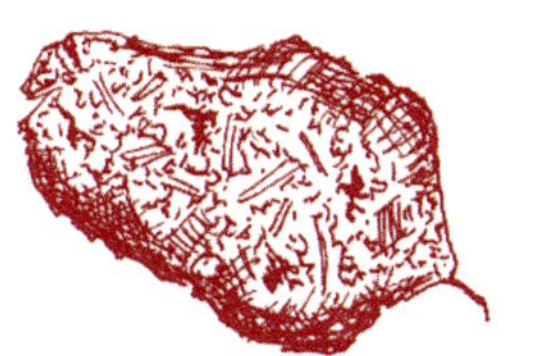

BEAVER

DIAMETER 1.8 cm
LENGTH 2.7 cm

Beaver scat is always filled with tiny bits of wood.
It is rare to find this scat since it's usually in water.

Muskrats mark their territory
with lots of scat.

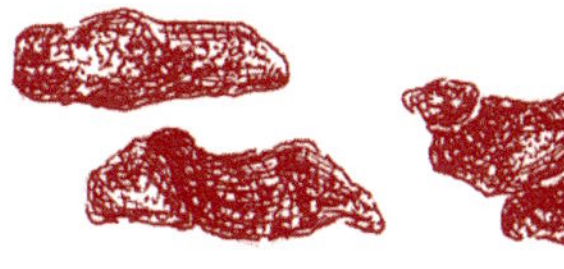

MUSKRAT

DIAMETER 0.5 cm
LENGTH 1.6 cm

 *Sphere*	*Elongated (Large)*	*Key ----- Page 29* 

PORCUPINE

DIAMETER 1.3 cm
LENGTH 2.0 cm

Porcupine scat is cashew-shaped and usually contains compacted wood bits. It is often found in piles.

Woodchuck scat is usually covered by dirt.

WOODCHUCK

DIAMETER 1.3 cm
LENGTH 3.0 cm

 *Sphere*	*Elongated (Large)*	*Key ----- Page 29* Ⓒ

Deer and Moose scat are usually found in piles.

DEER

DIAMETER 0.8 cm
LENGTH 1.3 cm

MOOSE

DIAMETER 1.5 cm
LENGTH 2.8 cm

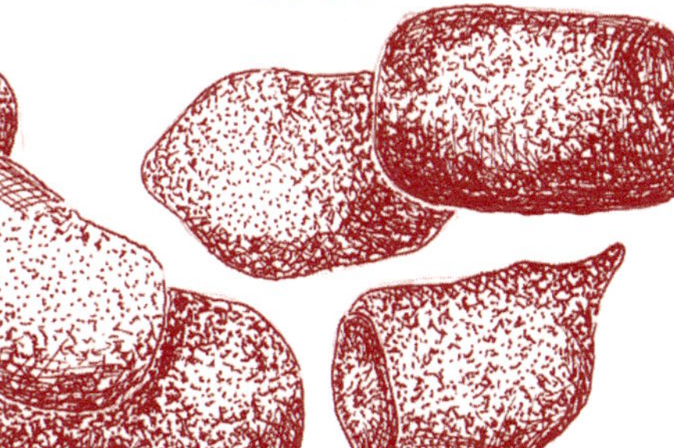

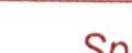 Sphere	Elongated (Large)	Key ----- Page 29 Ⓒ

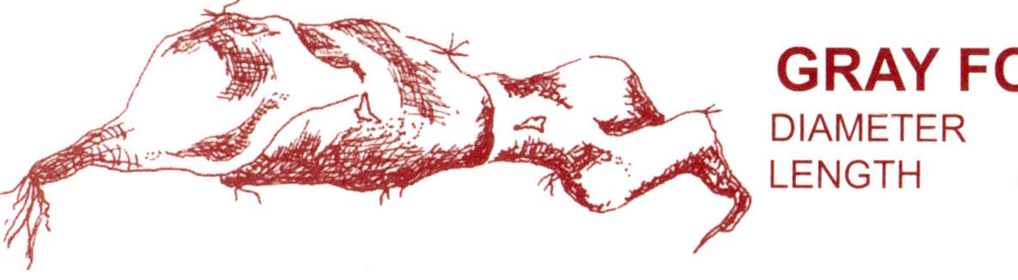

GRAY FOX

DIAMETER 1.5 cm
LENGTH 5.0 cm

RED FOX

DIAMETER 1.5 cm
LENGTH 5.0 cm

Red fox urine smells like a skunk.

Cylinder	Pointy	Key ----- Page 29 (D)

Key ----- Page 29 (D)

Coyote scat may contain larger pieces of bones, as compared to bobcat scat.

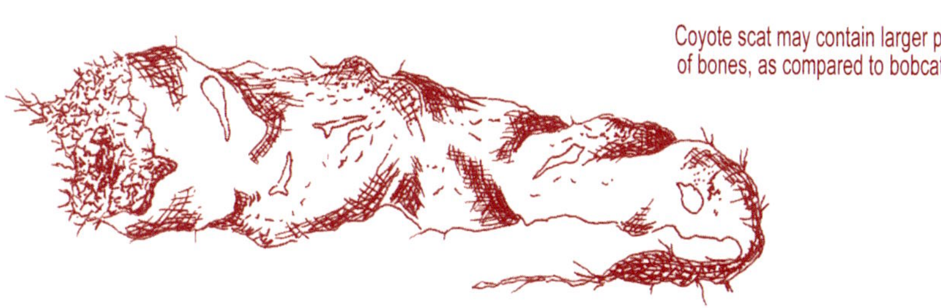

COYOTE

DIAMETER 1.9 cm
LENGTH 8.0 cm

 Cylinder	Pointy	Key ----- Page 29 (D)

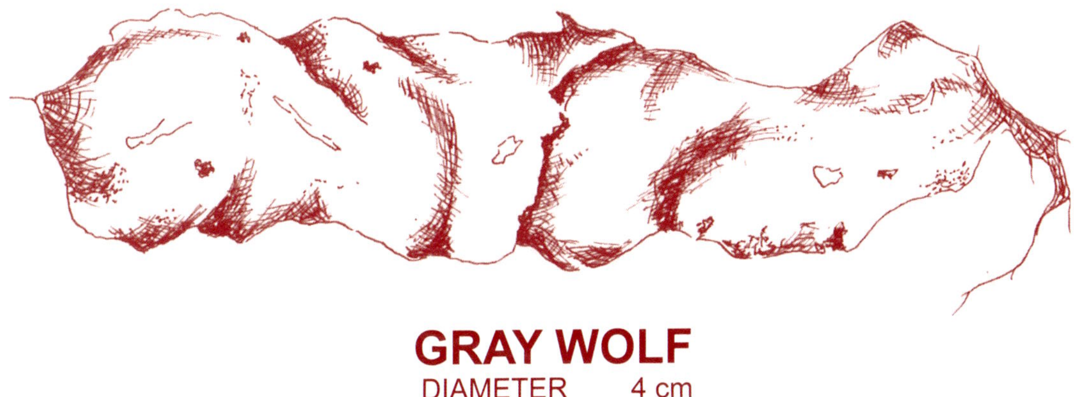

GRAY WOLF

DIAMETER	4 cm
LENGTH	15 cm

Cylinder	Pointy	Key ----- Page 29 (D)

Bobcat scat usually contains small pieces of bone.

BOBCAT

DIAMETER 2.0 cm
LENGTH 10.0 cm

MOUNTAIN LION

DIAMETER 4.0 cm
LENGTH 10.0 cm

Cylinder	Broken	Key ----- Page 29 (E)

WEASEL

DIAMETER 0.3 cm
LENGTH 3.5 cm

MINK

DIAMETER 0.6 cm
LENGTH 5.0 cm

MARTEN

DIAMETER 0.6 cm
LENGTH 5.0 cm

Fisher scat contains coarser hair than weasel, mink or marten scat.

FISHER

DIAMETER 1.2 cm
LENGTH 9.0 cm

Cylinder	Twisted	Key ----- Page 29 (F)

RACCOON

DIAMETER 1.7 cm
LENGTH 7.5 cm

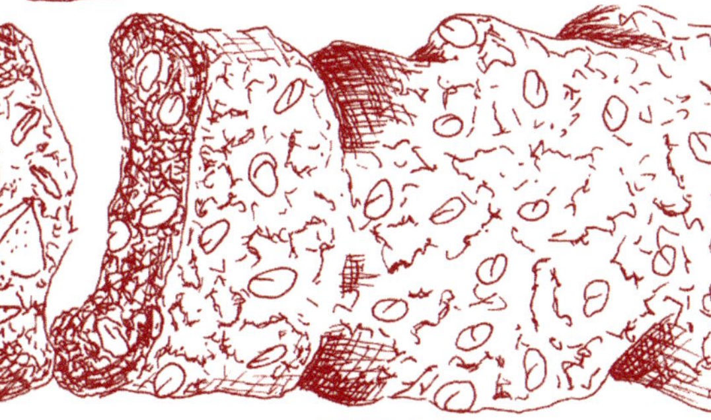

BEAR

DIAMETER 3.5 cm
LENGTH 16.0 cm

Raccoon and Bear scat often have seeds, pits or nut shells..

 *Cylinder*	*Blunt*	*Key ----- Page 29* Ⓖ

OPOSSUM

DIAMETER 1.3 cm
LENGTH 10.0 cm

SKUNK

DIAMETER 1.9 cm
LENGTH 8.0 cm

Skunk scat usually contains insect fragments.

Cylinder	Miscellaneous	Key ----- Page 29 (H)

Otter scat usually contains fish scales and bones.

OTTER

DIAMETER	2.5 cm
LENGTH	12.5 cm

 Cylinder	Miscellaneous	*Key ----- Page 29* (H)